ONE WAY

A Trip With Traffic Signs

Leonard Shortall

STOP

SLIPPERY WHEN WET

STAY IN LINE

Prentice-Hall, Inc., Englewood Cliffs, N.J.

Printed in the United States of America   J

Prentice-Hall International, Inc., London
Prentice-Hall of Australia, Pty. Ltd., North Sydney
Prentice-Hall of Canada, Ltd., Toronto
Prentice-Hall of India Private Ltd., New Delhi
Prentice-Hall of Japan, Inc., Tokyo

Library of Congress Cataloging in Publication Data

Shortall, Leonard W
    One way.

    SUMMARY: Follows the comical travels of a car
through a maze of traffic and signs.
    [1. Traffic safety—Fiction] I. Title.
PZ7.S55878On   [E]   74–2281
ISBN 0–13–636159–5

"Goodbye!" "Have a nice trip!" It's a lovely day
For two cars to travel along one way.

Stop at the sign, look left and right
Wait for the cars to pass, be safe and polite.

Stop again while the bears cross by the school
We'll wait without beeping — that is the rule.

Detour! The car wobbles and thumps
They're digging and paving to smooth out the bumps.

We yield to the cyclists, though we hate to wait
With all of this traffic, we're going to be late.

It's dark in the tunnel and scary — oh my!
Take off your glasses and see what went by.

REMOVE
SUN
GLASSES

TUNNEL

Dear me! What a line! We'll have to stop here
Says the doe to her fawn — "After you, deer."

"I think it's raining, I feel a drop!"
"Pull over, friend, and we'll put up the top."

The bridge up ahead is not very wide
There's not an inch to spare on either side.

The funny old plane swoops like a bird,
It's the noisiest thing I've ever heard!

"Let's picnic here, this rest stop looks best
Then you can drive and I'll take a rest."

"The country's so pretty, just look at the view…"
Keep your eyes on the road, whatever you do!

Look who's beside us, it's hard not to stare..."
Oops, we'll remember to drive on with care.

Down with a bang comes the black and white gate
We can count the train's cars while we sit here and wait.

Uh, oh, the tire is flat,
A jack and a lug wrench will take care of that.

A good safe trip on the Fourth of July
Start up the fireworks and light up the sky!